Grief Songs

Elizabeth Gauffreau

Paul Stream press
Nottingham, NH

Images: Gauffreau Family Collection

Acknowledgement: "Grief Song" was first published in *Cleaning Up Glitter,* April 2019, Volume 1, Issue 1.

Please direct inquiries to:
Paul Stream Press, LLC
49 Smoke Street
Nottingham, NH 03290
contact@paulstreampress.com

Library of Congress Control Number (LCCN): 2020919600

ISBN: 978-1-7359292-0-0

Past as the days that set,
While only one remembers
And all the rest forget, –
But one remembers yet.
~ Christina Rossetti

Elliott Francis Gauffreau
April 27, 1924 – March 15, 2000

Katharine Elizabeth Brown Gauffreau
August 5, 1930 – November 2, 2019

George Leon Gauffreau
August 29, 1957 – November 30, 2017

CONTENTS

GRIEF SONGS

Grief Song

GAUFFREAU
BELOVED HUSBAND
FATHER AND G-DA
GEORGE L.
AUG 29 1957 – NOV 30 2017
FOREVER IN OUR HEARTS

God has had him long enough
the Innocent cries
send him home at once
God has no say in the matter
the Experienced replies
God cannot oblige
and from the Poet
the images fly
he's here in glimmering water
he's here in shimmering sky
but Poetry has no say in the matter
poetry cannot oblige

Grief Song II: This

this wasn't supposed to happen
this final indignity
this querulous voice
this hollow-eyed stare
this startled shuffle
this bemused bobble
this timorous tremor
this unreasoning hope
for life

Grief Song III

I held her hand
as she lay dying
death rattle
in my throat

POEMS OF LOVE & REMEMBRANCE

WRITTEN IN TANKA

In the Wilderness

snowy wilderness
cold winter sun, soaring trees
a small lone figure
for a time she stood fearless
my protector, my mother

27 Edgewood Road

clearing out the house
entering forbidden rooms
hidden photographs
baby picture never seen
her pride in me now showing

A Goodwill Love Story

Goodwill summer camp
children deloused, chance meeting
Thanksgiving formal
engagement ring at Christmas
first in her class to marry

WWII Enlistment

joined up after school
a skinny kid with glasses
relentless heat, rot
the jungles of New Guinea
a damn sight better than home

The Dance

thirty years married
dancing at George's wedding
I out of the frame
failed marriage foreseen, still
I did not begrudge them the dance

At the Cottage

pensive eyes downcast
salt-laden breeze, bird racket
second pregnancy
birds devour chokecherries
before long spoiling the lawn

VACCINATION DAY

perched on mother's lap
two children unsuspecting
needle pricks to scar
tiny table, bent wire chairs
root beer floats a mother's love

On the Porch

brother and sister
brave howling winds, snow’s cruel bite
safely on the porch
snowsuit swish, smile for Daddy
no memory of that day

To Write a Sermon

a two-year-old knows
nothing of homiletics
words into ether
pencil paper fine motor
oh the places she will go

ANGELIC

his precious angels
Daddy’s favorite portrait
little did he know
George had cried piteous tears
while I railed against my bangs

Youth Group Picnic

I still remember
George and I out of the frame
waiting for Daddy
honk, giggle, honk, giggle, honk
dead battery, pop the clutch

Time

nightly ritual
strategic choice of story
Daddy called it Time
wait till your father gets home
not a threat but a promise

TIME MACHINE

silly school project
cardboard box, green poster paint
George's time machine
trips through time at his command
if only he had kept it

Confirmation Day

catechism first
cartoon people contemplate
sacrament and such
eucharistic alchemy
more time with Daddy for me

First Sacrament

seminarian
drives four hours through the snow
daughter's sacrament
mother rocks her as she cries
prays the car stays on the road

BAPTISM

fearsome marble font
echoes hollow ritual
tender droplets fall
just enough for sacrament
soft kiss for baby's forehead

Boy Scout Badge

walk a dusty road
distance meritorious
no badge without proof
Daddy matched him step for step
hot August sun beating down

Clam Bake

clam bake on the beach
driftwood fire crackles, smokes
Michael row the boat
Mummy sings, guitar strumming
five hundred miles from our home

Beach Day

Panda, Lulubelle
Mummy, George, and I of course
warm sand memory
just Lulubelle and I now
detritus of a beach day

Another Beach Day

brother and sister
on the beach, wind, sea spray, smiles
no diagnosis
his arm around her shoulders
the sand firm beneath their feet

Yearbook

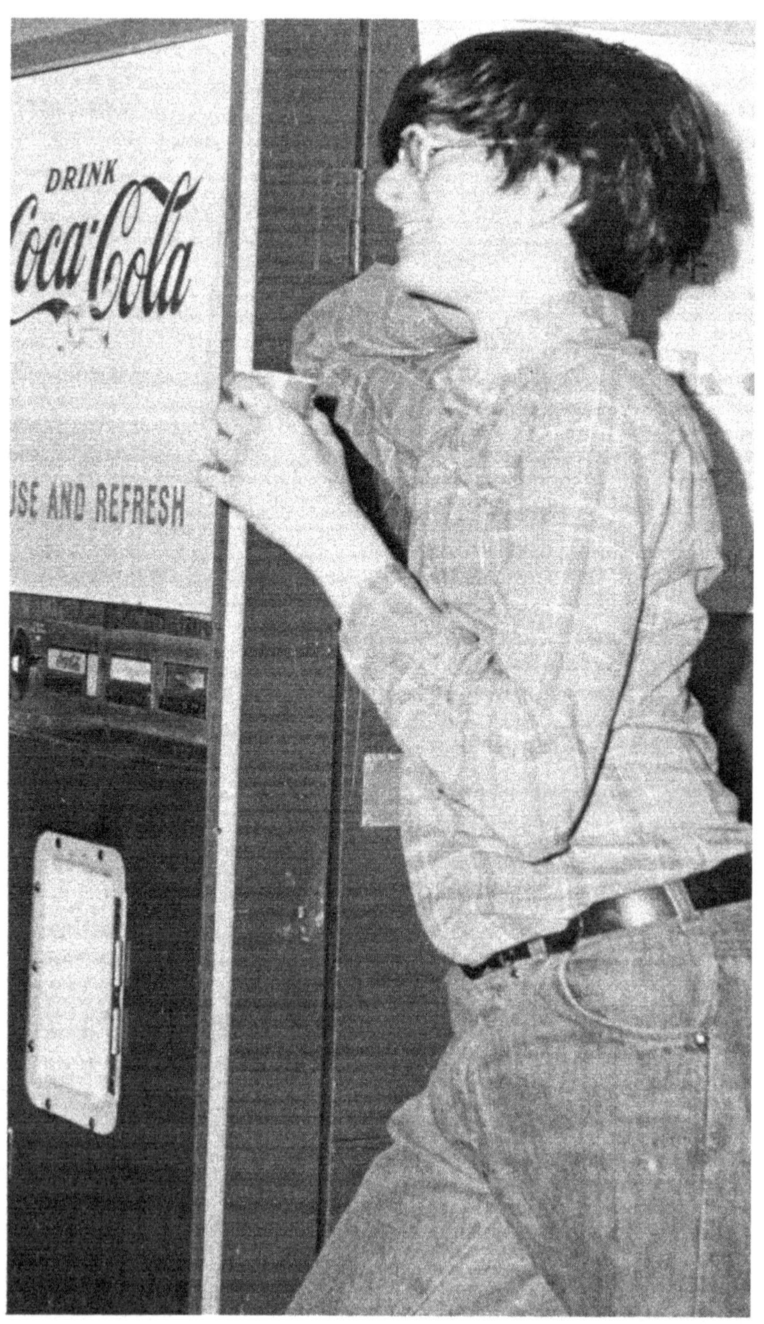

see George strike a pose
Coke machine, casual lean
no caption needed
George Gauffreau enjoys a Coke
classmate, friend, brother, deceased

For a Crooked Smile

oh, that crooked smile
he was my little brother
teller of tall tales
he smiled for me one last time
around the tube in his throat

TURNING POINT

Berlin, New Hampshire
weight of the parish shouldered
forsake the petty
embrace the sick, the dying
succor accepted at last

Another Crooked Smile

oh, that crooked smile
indulging childhood foibles
memory unmoors
joyful smile, new homecoming
when I sit down to breakfast

The Vow

four a.m. phone call
sunny hospital alcove
tacit vow broken
guilt and regret unspoken
his forgiveness unwitting

Sixty Years of Katharine

sixty years safe under glass
minutes tucked into envelopes
decades left in dresser drawers
held in thrall, left behind
her blue eyes bright with wonder

Family Reunion

we did not expect
Indian summer so soon
early morning sun
haze lifts, mountain range appears
but only for a moment

Portland Head Autumnal

gray waters roiling
under a lowering sky
childhood waves bright blue
gold autumnal perspective
a pink rose blooms still open

WOULD YOU CONSIDER LEAVING A REVIEW?

If you think *Grief Songs* would resonate with other readers, please consider writing a brief review to let them know. I would be ever so grateful. Thank you!

GOODREADS:

https://www.goodreads.com/review/new/58328057-grief-songs

"Poetry is the revelation of a feeling that the poet believes to be interior and personal but which the reader recognizes as his own."
~Salvatore Quasimodo

CONNECT WITH LIZ

WEBSITE:
http://lizgauffreau.com

AMAZON AUTHOR'S PAGE:
amazon.com/author/elizabethgauffreau

BOOKBUB:
https://www.bookbub.com/profile/elizabeth-gauffreau

GOODREADS:
https://www.goodreads.com/egauffreau

POETS & WRITERS DIRECTORY:
https://www.pw.org/node/1079971

FACEBOOK:
https://www.Facebook.com/ElizabethGauffreau

LINKEDIN:
https://www.linkedin.com/in/liz-gauffreau

TWITTER:
https://twitter.com/LGauffreau

About the Author

Elizabeth Gauffreau writes fiction and poetry with a strong connection to family and place. She holds a B.A. in English from Old Dominion University and an M.A. in English/Fiction Writing from the University of New Hampshire. She is currently the Assistant Dean of Curriculum & Assessment for Champlain College Online, where she is an Associate Professor. Her fiction and poetry have been published in literary magazines and several themed anthologies. Her debut novel, *Telling Sonny,* was published by Adelaide Books in 2018. Liz lives in Nottingham, New Hampshire with her husband.

ALSO BY ELIZABETH GAUFFREAU

PRAISE FOR TELLING SONNY: GOODREADS

"This novel is beautifully written with a gentle pace but is still a page turner as the reader becomes fascinated in how the story of this ill-fated relationship is going to end. Thankfully, the author provides us with secret revealing final chapters, as the story of Faby, Louis, and Sonny the child they share, comes to a close. Highly recommended."

"Her coming of age is painful yet tempered by a bittersweet revelation at the end that brought tears to my eyes."

" . . . the strength of the characters is one of the irresistible aspects of this well-crafted novel."

"I finished this book in record time, trying (and failing) to slow down so the story would last longer."

"Poignant and beautifully written. I highly recommend this remarkable novel."

"All in all, a beautifully written, evocative, sad, and curiously happy story I will remember for a long time to come."

"Gauffreau manages to recreate a lost world of 1920s small-town New England, Atlantic City, the vaudeville circuit, and rail travel. She obviously painstakingly researched the novel, polishing every detail of each scene until it shines with clarity. Gauffreau's writing style successfully marries the direct nature of contemporary writing with a more graceful syntax that befits the time period, as well as Faby's upbringing."

"*Telling Sonny* by Elizabeth Gauffreau is a sweet, lovely, insightful, and compelling novel, and I give it my highest recommendation."

CPSIA information can be obtained
at www.ICGtesting.com
Printed in the USA
LVHW011622231021
701314LV00020B/1060

9 781735 929200